A Beginner's Guide On How To Feel, See & Strengthen The Auric Field

By Luna Sidana

Table Of Contents

Introduction 1

Chapter 1: What Are Auras? 4

Chapter 2: Auras In Different Traditions 15

Chapter 3: Layers 23

Chapter 4: The Colors & Shades 32

Chapter 5: How To Sense Auras 45

Chapter 6: How To See Auras 54

Chapter 7: Perceiving Your Own Aura 61

Chapter 8: Cleansing & Protecting 69

Chapter 9: Strength & Health 86

Conclusion 101

© **Copyright 2017 by Pine Peak Publishing**

- All rights reserved -

In no way is it legal to reproduce, duplicate, or transmit any part of this document in either electronic means or in printed format. Recording of this publication is strictly prohibited and any storage of this document is not allowed unless with written permission from the publisher. All rights reserved.

The information provided herein is stated to be truthful and consistent, in that any liability, in terms of inattention or otherwise, by any usage or abuse of any policies, processes, or directions contained within is the solitary and utter responsibility of the recipient reader.
Under no circumstances will any legal responsibility or blame be held against the publisher for any reparation, damages, or monetary loss due to the information herein, either directly or indirectly.

This document is geared towards providing exact and reliable information in regards to the topic and issue covered. The publication is sold with the idea that the publisher is not required to render accounting, officially permitted, or otherwise, qualified services. If advice is necessary, legal or professional, a practiced individual in the profession should be ordered.

Respective authors own all copyrights not held by the publisher.
The information herein is offered for informational purposes solely, and is universal as so. The presentation of the information is without contract or any type of guarantee assurance.

The trademarks that are used are without any consent, and the publication of the trademark is without permission or backing by the trademark owner. All trademarks and brands within this book are for clarifying purposes only and are the owned by the owners themselves, not affiliated with this document.

Introduction

The most agreed upon origins of the word "aura" can be traced back to Greek and Latin roots with the meanings "breeze", "breath", "wind" or "air". In the mid-19th century, the term started to take on a different connotation in Europe, and was used to describe the "characteristic impression" made by a person.

A few years later, spiritualists adopted it to convey the subtle field of energy that radiates off beings. Hindu scholars insist that "aura" actually comes from Sanskrit, and refers to the spokes in a wheel. The imagery of a spoke originating from a hub is a parallel to how the aura radiates from the physical body.

At any rate, "aura" has made its way into mainstream language, and is used to indicate something that is both palpable, yet simultaneously intangible. It describes the mood or ambiance of a person, place, thing, or situation. People talk about how someone has an aura of happiness, gloom, anger, fear, or even mischief.

Similarly, a place can be said to have a certain kind of atmosphere, and even events can take on their own personality (i.e. "The ritual had an aura of mystery"). It is a way of expressing how something *feels* and the energy that is emitted from it, rather than describing it in terms of physical characteristics and other concrete, solid ways.

It is also understood that the aura of something changes depending upon circumstances; a person who usually has a sunny disposition may surprise her friends with her uncharacteristic vibe of doom and gloom after receiving bad news.

Interestingly, "aura" is utilized in modern medicine to describe symptoms that precede the onset of specific neurological conditions, such as epileptic seizures or migraines. Patients may experience a rush of coldness or see pulsating lights prior to an attack. The nature of both this linguistic mechanism, as well as the unusual physical ailments, points to the fact that auras are indicators of finer levels of experience.

Chapter 1:

What Are Auras?

Modern science is proving that matter is not solid. In the most fundamental sense, the universe appears to be composed of light and sound waves. What appears to be firm and "real" is actually a pulsating mass of protons, electrons, neutrons, and even *smaller* particles. These particles vibrate in a specific way, and the corresponding frequency determines physical characteristics such as weight, size, shape, color, texture and so on and so forth.

Everything is made of energy, and the energy itself is neutral. It is capable of becoming anything, depending on the way in which it vibrates, and is plastic in nature. Electrical impulses are generated in the body by the friction of these particles, and this vibration creates a magnetic field — a principle that is upheld by the laws of physics. Hence, any body with electrical impulses automatically incurs a magnetic field; another name for this field is "aura"

Auras have been recognized worldwide and throughout history as three-dimensional, oval, egg-shaped fields of electromagnetic energy that surround all living and nonliving things. Mystics and other clairvoyants have long described this phenomenon, often describing them as waves and bands of colors radiating out from the subject of observation. Halos depicted in religious iconography are another way of portraying this curiosity.

People under the influence of LSD, mushrooms, ayahuasca, peyote, and other substances frequently describe so-called hallucinations that closely resemble the descriptions made by mystics in meditative states. Some spiritual practitioners use hallucinogens to induce these trances, in which auras and other forms of energy become visible.

People on their deathbeds, or who have had near death experiences, often recount the radiance surrounding different souls. The aura is only present in physical forms animated by life; a corpse will not have an aura, but a ghost will.

Over time, especially in the West, there has been a

rejection of the esoteric, in preference for scientific methods that come to conclusions based on what is observable and measurable with the five senses. Yet even when societies moved away from an esoteric understanding of the body, there were always those who were not content with mainstream information.

The medieval Swiss-German physician Paracelsus believed the education, particularly medicine, taught at the time in the universities was incomplete. He stated that a doctor should seek the counsel of, "old wives, gypsies, sorcerers, wandering tribes, old robbers, and such outlaws" to learn what was really necessary. He also came to the conclusion that the human aura was a reality. He said, "The vital fluid is not inclosed in man, but radiated round him like a luminous sphere."

More recently, technological advances like Kirlian photography have captured these fields and made them apparent to anyone, while other forms of paranormal research continue in small circles. Still, there are skeptics who do not believe in the existence of auras and other metaphysical phenomena, and claim the accounts are nothing more than an abnormality in the brain's functioning, a symptom of mental illness, or simply an overactive imagination.

Western style experiments consistently produce mixed results in the attempt to "prove" various metaphysical truths. This can, however be explained in metaphysical terms: It is impossible to come to a firm conclusion when the fluctuating states of reality (that which is perceived with the five senses) is being used as a basis for experimentation.

These states are constantly changing, and mask the true laws of the universe that never change, and exist under the distorted perceptions of mankind.

This is the difference between ancient, energetic medicine that never changes, and modern medicine that changes its mind every few years on whether or not eating this or that is good for our health. The other principle is "truth reveals itself to sincere seekers, not doubters". There are now numerous studies that support what the ancients have been saying for ages.

Some people can see auras, and others can feel them

without clear visuals. But all are aware of them on the level of intuition. It is common knowledge that we assess a person by how they "feel", and often know quickly whether or not we will get along with another person. Many people know almost instantly that this new man or woman will become their life partner.

Even hardened skeptics will admit to this, and those uninterested in the subject matter are apt to have, at one point in time, talked about a feeling they had when they met a particular person. How many times have you heard, "There's something about him I just don't like"?

Many animals have a heightened ability to read auras and, unlike humans, do not hesitate to act on their instincts. There are pet owners who know they can trust a stranger if their dog is friendly to them, and sometimes an animal's behavior indicates that someone who's still out of sight is approaching.

Even commenting on what color suits a person is an indirect knowing of the aura. Someone looks great in particular colors because the color on their physical body complements the colors of their aura. Tones that clash with the aura look positively dreadful, and even seem to drain the wearer of wellbeing. Certain people are drawn to certain colors, and prefer the ones they feel comfortable in for a reason.

For the average person, the aura extends approximately three to five feet from the borders of the physical body. It is densest at the section closest to the flesh, and gradually becomes more transparent and indistinct the farther away it goes. It can be described as a cloud or flame that gradually fades out of the field of vision. The field is broader in a healthy person than in someone who is ill.

Also, more advanced souls have larger and stronger fields that can be several miles in diameter. These well-developed individuals have a bright radiance, while people existing at a base level will have dull, uninspired fields.

The aura contains emotional, physical, cognitive, and spiritual information about the person, and is essentially a reflection of the person's energetic composition. This includes their current life as well as past ones. The size and colors of the aura continuously fluctuate depending on the current state and health of the being, and can change significantly over time.

People with a lot of charisma have stronger fields, and have an ability to influence people with their power. People who are confident and healthy have more resilient auras, and are better at deflecting energy coming their way.

Those who are unsure of themselves and suffer from emotional and physical problems will have thinner auras, and struggle to defend themselves from external influences. In spite of these difference, the aura of an ordinary person, even healthy ones, is not very stable, and reflects the ever-changing moods and compulsive thinking common to humans.

It is only with great spiritual work that the aura becomes steady and unwavering — a reflection of the training of the mind. With greater awareness comes an understanding of the value of the aura, and the need to proactively protect oneself against negativity, the same way we protect ourselves against illness and weather conditions.

An aura can expand or shrink according to the type of interaction. In general, expanding auras indicate a more expansive, happier state of wellbeing, while retracting energy is a sign of shrinking back into oneself. A healthy aura will experience changes, but will have a more durable nature and be able to stay balanced in the midst of environmental difficulties.

The aura changes based upon numerous conditions, including health, weather, and other environmental stimuli, interpersonal interactions, thought patterns, emotions, and spiritual practice.

Another important factor is the movement of the planets. The position of the heavenly bodies affect all in subtle and sometimes not so subtle ways. The aura actually contains the individual's astrological blueprints, and different signs tend to have unique characteristics in their auras that reflect their underlying tendencies.

For example, a balanced Cancer is very intuitive, and will display the corresponding soft blue color in her aura. If out of alignment, the Cancer may be moody, and her field will appear a violent red. The planets affect these tendencies and traits, shifting the energy in the aura itself.

Most auras are relatively calm with bursts of activity, and are quite small in comparison to their potential. In general, positive auras attract and negative auras repel. An important exception to this rule is when manipulative people use deceit to appear attractive, when underneath they are operating from low motivations. They are able to wear a kind of energetic mask that fool others into believing them, unless they are attuned to a deeper level of insight.

Other situations include feeling overwhelmed by a bright aura because it opens you up beyond your comfort zone, or being threatened by one because it reminds you of your own shortcomings.

Highly developed practitioners often attract the scorn, jealousy, and violence of lower vibrating life forms, and there is a history of saints around the globe being persecuted. An example of the impact of being in the proximity of a pure aura comes from a student of the "Bliss Permeated Mother of Bengal", an enlightened teacher from India.

According to her, the students were unable to tolerate being around "Ma" for extended periods of time. She said the guru's purity was so great that the rays from her field detoxified anyone in her presence. Her light forced out impurities in the followers' systems, and made their minds fill will all sorts of negative thoughts as they surfaced and were released. The disciple stated that most of the people excited to meet Ma did not stay long — they were forced to look at what lay inside, and it was more than they could handle.

Because the auric field extends beyond the earthly body, the auras of living being are constantly interacting and overlapping. Communication and exchanges of energy occur when this happens, and it is unavoidable unless you learn how to manage your energy. Some adepts keep their auras close to their sides for this reason.

Auras are extensions of individual souls, but it is possible for two or more auras to merge momentarily, temporarily, or for longer periods of time in a phenomenon called "auric coupling". Perhaps two friends had an in-depth conversation, or

two people were recently physically intimate.
It could also be a less ideal situation, for example merging with the other driver in a car accident or someone whom you consider an enemy. At these times, the auras share information more than in an ordinary interaction, and the other person's field will appear in the other.

This also occurs following work done between an energy healer and a patient. In this exchange, there is a definite transfer of vitality from the practitioner to the suffering, and sometimes the healer absorbs the sickness into her own aura, and has to discharge the negative energies later.

Chapter 2:
Auras In Different Traditions

Much of the data available via mainstream avenues about the aura is a fusion of information based on ancient wisdom and first-hand accounts from modern psychics, such as Doreen Virtue and Sylvia Browne, and other contemporary clairvoyants. This could be generically be described as "New Age", and can be quite helpful for many. However, studying the aura is nothing new, and much more detailed, scientific information is available in multiple esoteric traditions.

Some historical psychics, like the medical intuitive Edgar Cayce, established legitimate foundations dedicated to paranormal research. If we are to look back further in history, different schools of thought from all the major faiths speak about the aura, and some groups studied it intently. Whether or not the aura was emphasized is a matter of theoretical orientation. Some groups put a lot of time and energy into working with it, while others did not deem this as quite so important.

Studying the aura in mystical traditions was not a purely intellectual pursuit, or done to satisfy curiosity; It was performed with the aim to increase understanding of the self, and learn how to actively work with the energies of the body.

Most people live in a highly reactive state, and this is why the aura fluctuates so much in the majority of people. We live out life in response to events instead of training ourselves to find stillness in the midst of chaos and act from our core. The result is clear — we are happy when things are going well, and miserable when things are not.

Cultivating inner stability allows you to experience greater degrees of acceptance and peace, even during the most trying of circumstances. Simultaneously, it changes our vibration and attracts more favorable circumstances.

Ancients (and modern practitioners alike) understood that working with the aura enabled them to gather information about the nature of the human condition, and put them in proximity to higher states of bliss.

Perhaps the most well-known group of practitioners who work closely with the aura are the Tantric yogis, the most mystical and esoteric branch of Hinduism. The Tantric philosophy operates on the understanding that heaven and earth are extensions of the other, and the body itself is a microcosm of the universe. Because of this, having a healthy physical body is encouraged, and the energies of the body are mastered and transmuted.

It also means the body can be used as a suitable vehicle to higher consciousness in the form of yoga poses, breathing exercises, mudras, and, for a minority of Tantric practitioners, sex (In spite of Western sensationalism of what Tantra involves, the majority of Tantrikas are actually celibate).

Because Tantrikas say the physical body is a mini universe, the energetic anatomy has been painstakingly investigated and mapped out. Techniques have been developed to manipulate the energies in ways that benefit and speed up spiritual evolution. Working with the aura is definitely part of this.

"Aura" in Sanskrit is "prabhamandala" (meaning "luminous circle"), or "diptachakra" ("wheel of light"). The aura is composed of seven layers, and each layer corresponds to one of the major chakras.

There is an internationally recognized Buddhist flag made up of the colors of the Buddha's aura following enlightenment. Following his awakening, his aura contained blue, representing universal compassion; yellow for the Middle Path; red, depicting the five blessings that accompany the study of Buddhism; and white, which stands for purity. Together, they create a rainbow effect, and are referred to as "prabashvara". It is said that the Buddha's aura was approximately three miles in diameter near the end of his incarnation.

The Jains talk about how the aura of every individual has a specific color dependent upon that soul's karmas. The tone is dubbed "lesya", and can run the gamut of being a saintly white all the way to a black color that shows ignorance, hatred, and sin.

Tai chi masters and other martial arts experts work with the auric field as they explore the body's energy and learn to focus its power.

The descriptions of halos are perhaps the most obvious example of auras in more traditional Judeo-Christian sects. Religious iconography quite commonly depicts a bright or golden orb encircling the heads of divine beings, including prophets, angels, and other highly advanced mystics. Sometimes, the entire body has a radiant quality. The Bible describes how Jesus' face shone like the sun, and his robes became radiant during his transfiguration.

In Judaism, the Hebrew words for "halo" or "aura" are "hila" ("emanating light") and "ohr hamakif" ("enveloping light"). Like in the Christian tradition, halos can be seen surrounding righteous people of great faith, and the energy is especially potent around their faces, foreheads, and hands. The Torah describes how Moses' *hila* was so brilliant after coming down from Mt. Sinai that the people were blinded by its radiance. They couldn't even stand to look at him until he covered his face.

Ancient Jewish texts also describe how the fetus is surrounded by light while still in the womb. At this time, the soul is connected to higher planes of existence, and is in a very spiritual state — not yet fully established in the physical realm. This awareness of one's own inner divinity usually dims as more time is spent on earth. Some practitioners wear white garments on the Sabbath as symbols of strengthening the surrounding light of the "ohr hamakif".

Kabbalah, the mystical branch of this faith, works most extensively with the aura, and describes varying degrees of brightness and the different colors in the field that depend upon the person's closeness to God. Their philosophy on the aura and the discoveries they made about its nature is much the same as the Tantrikas from India. The Tree of Life is an important symbol in the kabalistic texts, and is used to represent how all life is interconnected and each being exists somewhere on it.

As taught by the Tantrikas, the human body is recognized by the Kabbalah as a mini-cosmos within itself, and the aura extends throughout different planes of reality — linking the individual with other individuals and the universe at large.

The aura is like a shell that surrounds the light of the soul, and the aura is responsible for maintaining and creating the physical body, as well as the vehicle for receiving and transmitting information to and from invisible worlds.

The inner layers of the aura closest to the physical body are the levels of consciousness closest to material reality on the earth plane. The outer layers correlate with higher realms and more refined levels of consciousness. In most people, the aura is smaller because the light fills the inner, but not outer layers.

A major component of spiritual work in Kabbalah is strengthening and expanding the aura in the effort to develop the degree of consciousness itself. With discipline, the apprentice learns how to control what energies are being absorbed, and how to direct the psychic matter for awakening and awareness.

Symbols and visualization techniques are heavily utilized to accomplish this.

Perhaps the newest wave studying the aura are the modern-day scientists. More and more physicists are coming up with findings that sound shockingly similar to wisdom that was recorded thousands of years ago. It supports the age-old notion that there is one truth, but many ways to arrive at it.

Chapter 3:

Layers

Different societies have described the layers of the aura, and all have a similar message — the auric field is composed of multiple layers, or bodies, and correspond to varying levels of consciousness. For simplicity and consistency, we will refer to the model outlined in Hindu texts, and use the corresponding terminology.

Energy, and life in general, can be broken down into two broad categories: gross and subtle, or visible and invisible. Gross, or visible energy is what most of us define as "the real world". It is the energy that characterizes the earth plane that can be perceived with the five senses. This includes our physical body, our homes, trees, roads, books, objects, etc., etc., etc.

Most people live their lives focusing solely on the physical realm perceived by the human sense organs, and think this is all that there is. However, once we start talking about feelings and thoughts, we are making our way into subtle territory.

Emotions and the mental process of thinking are also recognized as "real", but they are much more intangible and harder to define. Everyone experiences them, but seeing them in the same light as a piece of paper can be difficult. Paper is a concrete object that can be held.

You can't hold a feeling or thought. More importantly, most people disregard the power of these subtle mechanisms; Thoughts and feelings are often discounted as meager things that rattle about in our heads — surely, they cannot be terribly important, and cannot possibly affect the outcomes of our lives very much?... Can they?

According to metaphysics, we are multidimensional beings living a simultaneously exulted and mundane existence. Matter that exists at the physical level vibrates at the lowest rate and therefore appears solid. Other types of energy vibrate at faster rates and cannot be perceived with the five major senses of the physical body. Thoughts and feelings fit within this category.

Basically, the human system vibrates on both the gross and subtle planes of reality. Those who choose to put all their attention into material realm alone, will experience life at a lower frequency — farther away from the mysteries of the universe.

Those who embrace their inner divinity, however, will discover subtler and subtler parts of themselves, and gradually become aware of the magnificence of creation. Once again: The human body is a microcosm of the levels of the universe, starting at a gross level and gradually becoming finer and finer. Remember, subtle energy carries much more power than gross, and what manifests on the earthly plane appears in the subtle first.

The Subtle Bodies

The aura itself is composed of seven layers, or subtle "bodies".

1. The innermost layer is called the "etheric aura". It vibrates very close to the physical

body, extending 1.25-2 inches out from the earthly frame. It appears as shades of blue, or is whitish and almost colorless and is related to the root chakra. It contains information about the physical body and its health.

2. The next layer that pertains to the sacral chakra is the "emotional aura" that, like the name suggests, holds feelings. This section is 1 to 3 inches wide, and radiates a rainbow kaleidoscope of colors. Emotional blocks will make the colors dull and muddied, and problems with this area will inevitably affect the adjoining bodies if not corrected.

3. Next is the mental layer that extends 3 to 8 inches away from the body. This contains mental processes such as thoughts and ideas, and is connected to the solar plexus chakra. It is yellow in color.

4. The astral level follows, and is connected to the heart chakra. It is the first layer that serves as a bridge to spiritual development. It radiates out approximately a foot, and reflects

a rainbow spectrum of color in healthy individuals.

5. The fifth layer, the etheric template, contains the blueprints for the physical forms in the world. It extends two feet outwards, and is linked to the throat chakra. Colors in this body vary.

6. The celestial layer comes next, and is tied to the third eye chakra. Like the third eye, this body is a place of divine communication and feelings of universal love and compassion. It has a very joyful quality, and those whose energy extends to this shell will experience feelings of ecstasy.

   This body is very refined, is deeply connected to the spiritual realm, and can extend up to two and a half feet. It has a wonderful, shimmering quality and displays many pastel colors.

7. Last comes the ketheric template, which embraces all the other layers and holds them

together. This is the finest, most blissful layer that can extend to over three feet. It is composed of gold threads, and vibrates at the highest frequency of any of the bodies. It contains the life experiences of the soul, and is the gateway to merging with the divine and becoming one.

The Major Bodies

There is more than one way to describe the layers of the aura, and another model describes it in a similar, but varying fashion. In this model, it is said that there are three major bodies and five total bodies. The bodies are referred to as "koshas", or sheaths that enclose the soul. The sheaths fit inside one another like Russian nesting dolls, and each is a veil obscuring the light that lies within all of us.

The three major bodies (beginning with the heaviest vibrating at the slowest frequency to the lightest and fastest vibrating body) are the gross, subtle, and causal bodies. These bodies interlock and interact with one another, and are reflections of each other.

1. The gross body is the same as the physical body, and dissolves at death. A new gross body made of the five elements is acquired upon each new incarnation.

2. The subtle body contains three sheaths, and is composed of the astral body and the two layers of the mind. Feelings, passions, desires, and thoughts are found in the astral body. The next two bodies relate to different kinds of thought processes. The first level of the mind is related to simplistic thinking, and relates to concrete, factual thoughts like, "I work at a bank".

    The next layer of the mind is responsible for higher levels of thought and abstract reasoning. This is where philosophical questions arise, and man ponders the meaning of life. This body is very engaged during the dream state.

3. Finally, we have the causal body. This body is so fine and transparent it is barely palpable. It is also referred to as the "bliss body", as it is the final veil coming between the individual merging with cosmic consciousness.

   Because it is so close to the origins of creation, it easily takes in nourishment from the cosmos. This is where memories and experiences from current and past lives are stored, serving as a blueprint for future incarnations.

   In the majority of people, the causal body is poorly developed, and most are rarely aware of this state of consciousness. Highly evolved souls are very conscious of this body, however, and their energy extends into this field in their recognition of their inherently blissful nature.

It is said that people suffer because the bodies are out of alignment, and we are unaware of the bliss body. When we reorganize our energies and reestablish communication with the final sheath, happiness naturally arises.

The subtle and causal bodies accompany the soul from incarnation to incarnation, with the goal of (gradually or suddenly) shedding the bodies, to finally exist in a state of continual ecstasy as pure light.

Chapter 4:
The Colors & Shades

So far, we have established that the aura is composed of multiple colors, that different layers hold different colors, and that the colors fluctuate depending upon the energetic state of the individual. The colors of the aura can be further identified and analyzed to reveal what the precise mental processes are. Thoughts actually have color, and any given color found in a person's aura is an indication of the presence of that kind of cognition.

The aura primarily contains the colors of the rainbow, but also has metallics, black, white, brown, and grey. Within each color are multiple variations, including the intensity and brightness of the color. In general, people experiencing greater states of harmony have brighter, more pastel hues in their aura. The presence of darker, muddy tones indicates imbalance, illness, and/or emotional distress.

Like the color wheel, there are three main astral colors that produce the rest: red, yellow, and blue. These three are mixed to form the secondary colors of orange, green, and purple. The colors can be further combined to produce more and more tones, like olive and russet.

Black is an absence of color, and white is a harmonious merging of the rest of the colors. Adding black to a color creates a darker shade, while adding white makes a lighter tint. Technically, these are neutral colors.

The number of colors that can be created by blending the primary colors and adding white or black is infinite. It is not uncommon for colors to be mixed within the other, or for one color to be superimposed upon another. Seeing streaks or dots of one color in another shows coexisting mental processes.

Sometimes, conflicting tones appear to be fighting each other as the individual wages a mental battle with themselves. This struggle can cease with the introduction of a neutralizing color that comes with a new way of thinking.

Other times, clouds of black will mask brilliant colors underneath, and explosive flashes indicate agitation or conflict. Because the human mind is rarely at rest, the aura is in constant motion of shifting, changing, and merging colors. Fierce emotions produce swirls, and create flamelike structures extending beyond the aura.

Red is related to the physical body and the mental processes that go along with a physical existence. It pertains to health of the body, namely to circulation and the heart. A clear red can be positive, and indicates good health and vitality. Strong natural states like friendship and an appreciation for movement in the physical body glow nicely. If, however, these become tainted by base motives such as companionship with negative influences, the clean red becomes dark and convoluted.

Different red tones can mean either very positive or very negative things. The astral color of love is similar to crimson, and selfless love has the color of a rose. Righteous anger manifests as a brilliant scarlet, and other types of rage that are more selfish in nature have a dull and dark quality.

Yellow represents the intellectual side. It is connected to reasoning, logic, deduction, analysis, synthesis, etc., and can reflect high or low forms of cognition depending upon the tone. It has many shades and tints, and the clarity of the yellow varies greatly. Pure, untainted intellectual attainment gives off a golden yellow, and can be seen around the heads of great teachers. This is the golden halo that has been painted in many portraits of holy figures, like Jesus and the Buddha.

Apparently, this light is so strong that their students are sometimes able to catch a glimpse of the nimbus. Those souls who emanate such a strong and clear golden light are incredibly rare. Intelligent people (without the latter's degree of intellectual attainment) will display more ordinary yellow color.

Blue is a reflection of spiritual and religious tendencies. This color is produced when we are focused on devotion, high ideals, morality, altruism, and so on. It runs the spectrum of pure spiritual emotion to lesser forms of faith that are based in fear and superstition. In the latter, black is mixed into the blues until deep indigos are produced, and the spiritual merits all but disappear.

Light, clear blues mean high spirituality is present, and the golden halo of great teachers is bordered by this tint. Grayish blue says that a person's spirituality is ruled heavily by fear.

Orange is a mix of red and yellow, and therefore reflects both physical and intellectual qualities. The presence of orange is linked to intellectual ambition and the wanting to achieve self-mastery through willpower. If there is a great deal of red in the orange, then the desire for intellectual mastery includes arrogance and wanting to control others with this skill.

More benevolent motivations for mental self-discipline will have less red and more yellow. This shows a vital, thoughtful soul who is considerate of others.

Green, the combination of the intellectual and the spiritual, is the color in the middle of the astral color spectrum. Because of this, it is a balance of the two extremes and is affected by both poles. The result is that the greens make sometimes surprising combinations. Clear, light green is a sign of charity, sympathy, and selflessness.

Other pleasant greens signify the individual's love of nature and being outdoors. Emerald green is the color of a healer, and is found in small amounts of people of this inclination.

A different shade of green shows tolerance for the views of others, but nastier shades of green can indicate quite distasteful mental states. Duller and duller tones increasingly reflect traits such as dishonesty, deceptiveness, and a lack of sincerity. Murky greens are signs of jealousy and envy. With this in mind, it is interesting to note that Shakespeare dubbed jealousy the "green eyed monster".

Purple is the color found in seekers of religious experiences or causes. This color often turns back to blue when they become set in their beliefs and career. A mixture of the earthly and spiritual, it is logical that purple is related to the love of ritual, form, and ceremony. This is especially accurate in regards to those holding religious office, or participating in

some sort of elaborate, regal ceremonies.
The highest spiritual vibration appears as violet. Wholesome religious feelings and pure existential thought show up in this way.

Brown indicates a desire for gain. Clear browns show an honest, industrious want for success, while murkier shades signify greed, stinginess, and covetousness.

Gray is an unpleasant color that is a sign of a lack of harmony. Grays mean there are negative emotions present, such as depression, anxiety, fear, timidity, and negativity.

White is, quite simply, pure spirit and the positive polarity of being. The use of white light in meditations and other esoteric methods is reaching towards the ultimate goal: To become white light itself. White goes beyond all the other colors, and transcends both the earthly and subtle plains as well.

Having white mixed in the human aura is very positive, and points to high levels of spiritual accomplishment. A white aura is a sign of being a

Master. Adding white to the other colors purifies them and increases their vibration.

Black is the negative pole of life and the opposite of pure spirit. Put very simply: It is hate. It dims the other colors when mixed together, and transforms them into baser qualities. Black means pessimism, depression, hopelessness, and evil.

Another important piece of information is this: Every individual has two basic ways in which the aura is colored. The person's underlying character will have a specific color profile that is based in habitual thoughts, feelings, and behaviors. This profile is more permanent in nature, and could be described as a person's "vibe", or personality.

Simultaneously, the soul is reacting to ever changing circumstances, and the passing thoughts and feelings are also present in the aura.

For example, a person of high moral character may tend to radiate pleasant blues. However, if the person is going through a difficult time, there will be other less desirable colors present, maybe grays and blacks.

The opposite is true when someone with a low character does a good deed, or thinks about something that makes him feel love. Trained mystics will understand this, and be able to discern the difference between the two.

Auric colors are not limited to living things. Places develop their own aura, or "astral atmosphere" based upon the interactions of individual within the boundaries. Everyone knows that some places have "good energy" and other places have "bad energy" depending upon what has happened there.

This creates its own web of colors — felt by many, visible to fewer. It is not difficult to imagine a tapestry of lovely colors hovering over a wonderful spot, and horrible, dark colors permeating a place that gives you the creeps.

A curiosity related to the phenomenon of the aura is the presence of thought forms. Like the aura, thoughts are vibrations, and made out of the same substance as the aura itself. The big difference between a thought and a thought form is the strength of the thought.

Most thoughts are transitory and relatively weak, but thought forms are created with much more force. Because of this, thought forms are surrounded by the vital energy of the thinker, and almost have a life of their own.

These thought forms have unique traits, like shape and color, based on the nature of the thought. They are created when the person has a strong feeling, idea, or passion, and a vortex is created within the aura by virtue of will power. The thought form may linger in the aura for a time and gradually fade, or stay strongly in the field for some time. In this case, the thought has the power to greatly influence other people in the vicinity.

If the thought form is strong enough, it can actually exit the person's aura and travel through space, affecting those who come into contact with it until it fizzles out, like the lingering vibration of a drum after the music stops.

Thought forms can manifest in many, many ways depending upon the individual's personality and the type of thought form being produced. The simplest and most common structure is that of small waves. Others look like clouds of smoke, rotating pinwheels, or jets of steam — some flying straight through the air, and others twisting and turning as they travel through space.

Thought forms originating from volatile emotions visually resemble the detonation of a bomb, blowing up once it reaches the person it is intended for.

Most of us have had this experience when someone who has been angry with us has forcefully directed his rage in our direction. These conditions can be more favorable, such as feeling a blast from an impassioned speaker.

People with the desire to persuade or manipulate send out grasping thought forms that can encircle the audience, as it attempts to pull the receiver towards the sender and what the sender wants. The thought forms can travel long distances, and the more focused the mind, the farther the thought form can go.

Because the thought forms are made of the same material as the aura, they also have colors, and are subject to the same system of color classification. The colors of thought forms are less intense, simpler, and less blended because they originate from a specific thought or emotion rather than a fluctuating mix of existence. People who can see auras may see thought forms as well, both within a person's psychic atmosphere and as they travel through space.

When color is described in such a way, it is easy to understand the concepts behind color therapy. It has been known for many years that stimulating colors should be avoided in places such as prisons and psychiatric wards. In general, red excites and warms the mind and body, yellow is stimulating and invigorating, and blue is cooling and soothing.

Ancient medical systems, such as Traditional Chinese Medicine and Ayurveda, use colors to balance the flow of energy. You, yourself, can work with the colors of the aura in the same way. It is based upon the simple principle that you summon what you focus your attention upon. Once you study the colors and feel comfortable with their characteristics, decide what you want to change about yourself. What colors do you want to radiate?

If your goal is to be a teacher or you want to stimulate your mind, visualize your aura awash in vibrant, bright yellows. If you want to feel love, surround yourself with rose hues. If there are things about yourself you do not like, choose a color that will replace your old way of being.

White can be added to colors you are aware of in your aura that could be purified. This can become very complex, so do not forget the cardinal rule of protection — encircling yourself with white light.

Chapter 5:
How To Sense Auras

The three following chapters will provide pragmatic tips and tools for becoming more aware of the auric field. You would be wise to use this information carefully. Developing psychic abilities can be a step towards greater insight and health. They can awaken wonderful things within us and give us a greater appreciation for the mystery of creation. However, it is good to be prudent and honest about your motivations.

Sometimes, people develop psychic powers when they are not grounded and stable enough to handle the doors they are opening. Instead of the information being a blessing, life becomes overwhelming and confusing; Too much information is not a good thing. Others deliberately develop clairvoyance for selfish or harmful motives, and psychic powers have a long history of being abused. Having psychic abilities does not always correspond with spiritual development. There are many psychics with remarkable talents who are not especially wise or advanced, and vice versa. Please use discretion when developing your skills and sharing these techniques with others.

It is also possible to have experienced unusual situations and be seeking explanations. Some people have intense experiences where they see or feel energy they were previously ignorant to, and don't know what to make of it. This can happen spontaneously or gradually.

Psychic abilities unfold naturally with spiritual practice as the self expands and the universe is discovered. The phenomenon can be magical or upsetting (sometimes both), and if it is causing you distress, learning how to live with it and controlling the ability is in your best interests. Researching the situation can be of great help, and sometimes, all you need is to know is that you are not crazy. Do not hesitate to contact a professional if you feel like you are in over your head.

An important consideration is whether or not others

allow their inner processes to be perceived. Being able to see or sense the energy in any given person, place, or object is an advanced skill. In general, other people must give you access to their energy to be able to perceive it, and the other party has the choice to block you, should they choose to do so.

Under these circumstances, you usually will not be able to see what you are wanting to, and will not be able to do so without consent. The exception is having a very good reason for obtaining the knowledge you seek or, in darker circumstances, disregarding the other person's requests and forcing your way into their energy.

As previously mentioned, it is normal for people to have a sense of the energy around them. In most people, it is relatively undeveloped, while others have excellent powers of intuition. Remember, each person is the same underneath; we are simply at different places along the journey. The subtle senses are latent in most, and anyone who has had contact with someone who has developed them will be staggered at what these people are able to perceive.

Children are often more likely than adults to have natural aura awareness. Because they are newer inhabitants to the planet and haven't forgotten where they came from, they frequently say things and report phenomenon that sounds peculiar to grown-ups.

Sensitive children may have strong reactions to certain people, warming up immediately to kind souls and refusing contact with negative ones. This behavior may be embarrassing to parents, but children are simply acting upon information they intuitively know to be accurate. They are sensing auric fields and, sometimes, even seeing them. This ability usually dims with age, as logic and appropriate social behavior take precedence. The good news is that the gift can be recovered, and even fine-tuned if one is dedicated enough.

When you practice any of these exercises, it is vital that you remain detached, and do not get involved on an emotional level. Once that happens, objectivity is lost, and it is hard to trust the accuracy of your perceptions. It is easy to get wrapped up in the experiences of others, or project your own thoughts and feelings onto them.

Let's begin with sensing the aura:

1. Begin by going to a place that makes you feel happy. Maybe it is a park, zoo, restaurant, or a family member's home.

2. Sit in your favorite spot and enjoy the feeling you get while you are there.

3. See what you notice and what you feel. Try to go beyond what your five senses perceive and *feel* the energy around you. You may want to close your eyes.

4. Try moving around the area, and see if you notice how the energy changes — maybe one spot is more positive or intense than the other.

5. Now walk away from your oasis and feel how the energy changes with the environment. What do you perceive?

Another exercise involves sensing the energy of other people:

1. If you have individuals in your life with similar interests (or a few folks willing to humor you), bring one of them with you. Find a quiet, roomy place where you know you will not be interrupted.

2. Have your partner stand on one side of the area, at least six feet away.

3. Slowly approach your partner, and notice what you feel as you enter the aura — become very aware of your own internal sensations and processes. Most likely they will change as soon as the auras overlap and you receive information from your partner. Maybe you will begin to worry more, or feel an optimism you did not notice previously.

4. When you are done, compare notes and ask your partner what they experienced.

This can also be done blindly with small groups of people:

1. Stand on one side of a door or other partition.

2. Have another person stand on the other side for a few minutes.

3. The first person takes notes on what they sense.

4. Have the second person switch with other people in the group, each standing on the other side of the door for a few minutes.

5. At the end, the first person will see what they were accurately able to perceive. Everyone can take turns.

Using photographs to evoke emotional reactions is another useful tool to develop sensitivity:

1. Prepare a number of images that conjure up strong emotions. Think of pictures that are likely make a person feel happy (maybe a

sunny day in a beautiful place), sad (a funeral), angry (someone being bullied), playful (puppies or kittens playing), afraid (scenes of war), nervous (a person about to drop a tall stack of dishes he is trying to balance), and so on.

As a control, include neutral, ordinary images that few people would react to, like a spoon or toothbrush.

2. Now, one by one, show your partner the pictures.

3. Each person should keep notes on what they experienced to be compared when finished.

Objects can also be used in a similar fashion:

Start picking up different objects and see what you sense from them.

You may want to compare and contrast items with different kinds of vibrations. For example, you may want to pick up fresh vegetables, junk food, and something more neutral, like a pen. The produce will generate positive energy, full of life force, whereas the junk food will vibrate at a much lower frequency. The pen's energy will be less noticeable, and serves as a guidepost in the energetic spectrum.

A variation on this exercise is placing different objects in bags and trying to describe their energy blindly (This is an excellent way to attune yourself to certain tools with healing properties, like plants or stones). You could add an object of sentimental importance, like a photograph or wedding ring, to see if you can feel the emotion the object has absorbed.

Switching from sensory perception to extrasensory perception is a discipline. Some people will do well quickly, and other people will struggle to pick up on much of anything. It's okay. If this is something that is important to you, it will come with time, patience and practice.

Chapter 6:
How To See Auras

Seeing energy is a much more developed and refined sense. Many have caught a glimpse of it at some point, only to dismiss it as their mind playing tricks on them. They may have seen light, color, or a fuzzy field around a person's outline.

When you first begin to practice seeing auras, it usually begins by seeing what looks like mist and waves. Honing in on colors and other details will take a lot of time and practice for most. Those with a natural proclivity most likely developed their skill in previous incarnations.

The densest layer closest to the physical body is the easiest to see, and viewing a blueish or whitish haze is a typical place to start. The more subtle the layers are, the more fine-tuned your subtle sight must be. The sixth and seventh layers are visible to almost no one. The ability to detect them indicates a highly evolved spirit.

There are probably more individuals that can see auras than we realize. People often keep such details about themselves secret, in the fear that they will be labeled as "weird" or "unstable", and will be rejected or judged by their peers. Nonetheless, those who have this ability sometimes put it to good use.

One woman said that whenever someone told a lie, she would see a streak of "lemony-green" pass through their field, close to the head. She was a schoolteacher for many years, and her students were amazed at how easily she saw through their falsehoods.

To practice seeing auras, there are certain techniques that can train the eyes to register subtle information. One such technique involves using the peripheral vision:

1. Go into a room with a plant and dim the lights. Ideally the plant will be against a solid, light, neutral wall.

2. Look at the plant with your peripheral vision instead of viewing it directly. With repeated

practice, a misty outline will appear around the plant.

3. After this, you can move onto animals and humans.

Another variation is squinting:

1. Follow the same procedure, but instead of using the peripheral vision, softly squint and watch energy appear among the blurry line of vision.

2. If you have a willing participant, have him or her stand in front of a neutral colored wall or background, before altering your vision to register the field.

3. When examining people, look specifically around the hands, between the shoulders, neck, and head. These are places most easily visible and you should be able to see the energy pulsate.

Distorting your normal vision lies in the truth that we

are able to sense deeper things when we are less focused on the obvious ones. A similar principle applies to channeling auditory information — if you learn to listen to the empty space, suddenly you will hear what is normally inaudible.

Other techniques to see the aura includes the use of visual aids:

1. Paint or draw two different colored circles, each about the size of a golf ball.

2. Make them so that they are positioned horizontally at the same height, maybe an inch and a half apart.

3. In the middle of the two larger circles, put a small black dot.

4. Stare at the black dot for 30 seconds while keeping the colored spheres in the peripheral vision. If your attention is kept on the dot, the circles will appear to have an aura of the opposite color around them.

Another diagram asks the person to rapidly shift the eyes among five evenly spaced black dots, eventually leading to a hazy, colored eminence around the disks. Yet another involves visually tracing a simple black spiral on a white foreground in and out, out and in 4-6 times, pausing after the figure has been traced completely.

Like the previous exercises, the goal is to train the inner eye to see things it has forgotten how to by focusing the attention on things we usually don't.

The aura contains all the information of the soul and that particular soul's journey. Different people will be able to "read" a variety of information about a person by viewing their aura. Some may primarily see colors, whereas others will have visions of symbols pertinent to that person's life.

Past life events, future possibilities, your mission in life, the nature of your soul group, and how the divine works through you are all imprinted upon the auric field, as well as established patterns and current habits.

When learning to see auras, you may also see information belonging to other important people or beings in the individual's life. With practice, the inner eye opens, and a hidden world will be revealed. What started as a fuzzy outline will soon develop into clearer visuals and yield all sorts of information. The famous psychic Edgar Cayce said that he would see figures appear and disappear in the aura of the person he was talking to.

If a person made a statement that reflected past life conditioning, the figure of a Greek, Indian, Japanese, or other person would manifest in the field, corresponding to whichever life in which he cultivated that belief. He said in the course of a conversation, he would see maybe 6 or 8 of these former selves appear.

Cayce, who saw auras his whole life, viewed this as an inherent gift, and something that would eventually develop in all (This is supported by ancient texts of India and other lands that describe psychic abilities as the norm in more enlightened ages). He said being able to read auras would lay us bare to our fellow man — making malicious intent and deception impossible to hide.

He also said the aura gives warning signs about impending ill health, financial disaster, and other worries. With this knowledge, many potential problems could be prevented.

Chapter 7:

Perceiving Your Own Aura

Becoming aware of your own energy is often the most important and first step to take when seeking spiritual truths. Doing so is unlocking mysteries about yourself and the universe at large. Being self-aware is not common or even highly valued in most mainstream circles. Because of this lack of insight, most stay stuck in the same reactive patterns, year after year, decade after decade. The more sensitive soul, however, decides to look within, and be more mindful about the choices she makes.

Learning to sense and even see your own aura is another way of becoming aware of yourself. In doing so, you will make a series of discoveries. Being able to see the human field is awe-inspiring, and reinforces the truth that we are spiritual beings having a physical experience. You may be overwhelmed by the beautiful aspects of yourself, and marvel at frequencies that surprise you.

The other side of the coin is discovering things about yourself that are painful. Maybe you see vile flashes of color in your own aura, and are sickened by what this means. The hard truth is that we often need to confront our flaws to gain the desire to change them — so be prepared to both find gifts you never imagined you had, as well as accepting your stumbling blocks and limitations.

Learning to sense your own field requires a little bit of time, concentration, and a quiet room:

1. Sit calmly with a straight back, to ensure proper energetic flow.

2. Take a few moments to relax, either keeping the eyes open or softly closing them.

3. Become very aware of your skin and the borders of your physical body.

4. Mentally scan your frame from head to toe until you have a sense for your gross body in space.

5. Next, imagine what lies beyond the skin, hair, and nails. Try to feel the next layer, the etheric body, just beyond.

6. Turn your attention to this next level radiating out an inch or two from the body, and see what you can perceive.

With practice, you will become conscious of this body in a similar way you are aware of your physical body. Sensing the first layer is the easiest, so keep going and see if the other layers reveal themselves to you.

The energy of the aura is most easily felt in the palms or the tips of the fingers. Sensing the energy between your hands is another basic technique, and is especially useful for energy healers, or those aspiring to become one. It is also a great way to focus the mind, increase the flow of vital energy, and improve health and vitality.

There are several variations, and this next one comes from the Chinese martial art and mind-body exercise Tai Chi (Indeed, Tai Chi operates on a subtle level, and simply practicing this will help you understand energetic flow and make you more aware of your aura):

1. In a standing position, relax your body and mind.

2. Take the martial arts horse stance (feet parallel and wide apart, squatting down a few inches, torso straight, with arms hugging the body, elbows pulled back, and hands in fists just in front of your waist) for a minute or more.

3. Stand up straight, leaving horse stance, and relax.

4. Close your eyes and begin rubbing your hands together for a few seconds.

5. Now move your palms together and away from each other as if you were kneading a small beach ball.

6. Visualize gathering the *chi*, or life force energy, between your hands.

7. Squeeze the ball of chi 1-3 times a second, keeping your hands 6 to 24 inches apart. Do this for 2-4 minutes or until you begin to feel sensations in your hands.

It may be feel like it's tingling, vibrating, heated, or like a magnetic force repelling the hands apart. Some may have results the first time, and others may need to practice several times prior to feeling the energy.

Next up, this simple practice can help you actually see the aura around your hands in addition to feeling it:

1. Take two pieces of cardboard, one white and the other black.

2. Place both hands on the white piece first, and gently look beyond the hands and at the space between the fingers.

3. Within a minute, you should see a pulsating, grayish white haze around the hand.

4. Now try this with the black cardboard.

5. Using the squinting or peripheral gaze tactic mentioned earlier also works on yourself:

6. You can begin by looking at a finger or hand, or you can look in a mirror at yourself with a soft gaze.

7. If you are using a mirror, stand 4 to 8 inches away from it, and look at the space about 3 to 8 inches away from your head (Soft light is ideal and it is best if the background behind you is white or neutral).

8. You will see waves and even colors around your body.

A more concrete way to see your aura is through the previously mentioned "Kirlian photography". This method was discovered by accident in 1939 by Semyon Kirlian. He noticed that an object placed on the photographic plate would display the aura if exposed to a strong electrical field.

Though Kirlian was not the first scientist to work with electro-photography, the method bears his name today. Certain photographers work with this medium, and can be found at psychic fairs, metaphysical shops, and the like. With proper research and the right equipment, you can even take your own photographs!

It is not a bad idea to have your aura read by a clairvoyant as well. While this is not quite the same as seeing it for yourself, there are certain advantages (Note: Beware of con-artists. Use discernment). If the psychic is skilled, she may be able to accurately read things in your field that you would not be able to, while maintaining a neutral position. This can be a positive and illuminating step along the road to developing your own skills.

More drastic methods also exist that will open you up to experiencing energy in a new way. These should only be considered after you are fully familiar with their effects and the potential dangers involved.

Techniques such as fasting, sleep deprivation, vision quests, sweat lodges, light deprivation, ceremonial dance, walkabouts, song and music, psychoactive drugs, mystical incantations, meditation on sacred diagrams, exposure to the elements, and other rituals all serve to break down the barriers within the mind and expose you to the cosmos as it truly is.

These methods are riskier, require the supervision of a skilled practitioner or guiding spirit, and are designed for those who have prepared for intense experiences. People who undergo these ordeals often report elaborate visions and directly receive information about the nature of the universe.

Use your intuition and common sense when drawn to these more potent options, and listen well to the advice of those who have walked the path before you.

Chapter 8:

Cleansing & Protecting

Bathing and other healthy habits have been utilized for a long time to ensure that our physical bodies do not become bogged down by unnecessary material. We exfoliate our skin, clear our sinuses, purge our digestive tract, and use diuretics to eliminate excess fluid in the body. Regular detoxification regimes have gained popularity in recent years as an excellent way to promote health and prevent disease.

These methods operate on the very simple understanding that our bodies are like machines dealing with inputs and outputs. If we have too many inputs, a poor ability to assimilate inputs, and/or inadequate elimination of waste, the body will become overwhelmed with matter that gets in the way of optimal functioning.

Eventually, this leads to disease. Maintaining the health of the auric field works in much the same way.

When the aura is clear, one experiences excellent immunity, better stamina, healthy boundaries, and emotional and physical resilience. When it is not, people become sick easily, are fatigued, anxious, or depressed, have poor boundaries, and may feel invaded by external sources.

There are different kinds of energetic disturbances that create problems in the aura's functioning. The field can become stagnant as a result of repressed emotions and negative thoughts. It is also possible to be impacted by negative thoughts coming from other people. This can happen via absorption of negativity from one's environment, or it may be the result of receiving negative energy that is being directed towards oneself from others whom are harboring ill will.

The universe is abundant, and filled with all kinds of different beings — from our dimension of existence and beyond — who, just like humans, are benevolent, neutral, or malicious. Sometimes, these entities become stuck in, or connected to, our aura, and can therefore hamper our wellness.

The presence may be spiteful in nature, but not always; There are lost souls roaming the earth who attach to living people in search of hope, safety, and comfort. It is not uncommon for these souls to be friends or family members from this or previous incarnations. No matter the circumstances, such a union is ultimately unhealthy for both parties.

Environmental toxins and other pollutants harm the aura just like they harm the physical body, and sometimes past life memories and experiences are lodged in the field, preventing growth and health. The earth emits different kinds of frequencies, and earth energies such as the intersection of the Hartman and Curry grids can create problems. Even the presence of underground running water can slightly shift the energies in your body.

It is very easy to pick up excess, often negative, energy that clogs the system and prevents smooth functioning. Many people unknowingly go through life experiencing different kinds of stresses related to issues with their auras in varying degrees of intensity. This can happen to anyone, but it is more likely to cause significant problems in highly sensitive people.

These folks are prone to absorbing the energy in their environments like sponges, and can quickly and easily become overwhelmed. This dynamic creates both emotional and physical symptoms, and can lead to chronic conditions if not properly identified and treated.

It is important to understand that no one single person operates in isolation. All life is connected, and both mystics and physicists describe how every person shares currents of energy with the other. Ultimately, every little thing on this planet is cut from the same cloth.

All forms in the universe are splintered points of light, and being tied to every other form of life is simply the reality of existence. It is neither healthy nor unhealthy; it is what it is. However, humans create additional connections with other humans and life forms daily through interactions.

Energetic cords (which are similar to the function of the umbilical cord) and other connections appear when people interact and create attachments to others. These attachments become actual structures, and indicate a flowing of energy between two parties that can be either positive or negative in nature. The exchange can be mutually beneficial, mutually destructive, or good for one party and bad for the other.

The cords are more like a web in which we are attached to others via a connection with one person, ultimately reaching every soul on the planet. The cords are weak or strong depending on the nature of the relationship, and there are different types of cords depending upon the nature of the connection. The strength of a cord will vary in accordance with the strength of the relationship.

Most people's auras resemble pincushions — there are cords everywhere, which means an erratic giving and taking of energy with others. The majority of these connections are unnecessary, and cause disruption in one's wellness and peace. Negative cords can create significant disharmony. Clearing and protecting the aura includes removing cords that are not helpful.

Like most things in life, prevention is far preferable

to treatment. Thankfully, there are several simple ways to maintain the health of your field. Regular cleansing will increase clarity, stamina, and overall health.

Smudging.

The burning of specific dried plants with protective qualities has been used for ages around the world to cleanse a person's field of unwanted and unhealthy vibrations. The plants that have been prepared for this purpose are referred to as "smudge", and the process is simply called "smudging". It is a simple practice in which the smudge is lit, and then the smoke is fanned or waved around a person, object, or space to remove stagnant energy.

For extra protection, you can face and send the smoke in four directions. This should be done in a well-ventilated area, so that the cleansing smoke can escape. Sage is the most common smudge, but others include cedar, lavender, sweetgrass, frankincense, and myrrh. It is also a good idea to mentally and emotionally welcome in positive, new energy as the smudge is removing the old and unwanted.

Visualization

One of the simplest ways to clean and protect the aura is through determined visualization. Two popular methods are visualizing a protective bubble of energy around yourself, or mentally encircling your being with pure, white light.

If you choose, you may wish to imagine ushering in clean, positive, protective energy while simultaneously releasing any negative, stagnant energy stuck in your field. This can be done daily, and some people like to start their morning off with this intention.

Shielding

When you feel negative energy coming your way, find ways to block it! There are a number of techniques to choose from. You can visualize a shield that dissolves any negativity coming its way, or imagine negative vibrations harmlessly sliding off a protective bubble or cocoon. You can imagine an infinity sign in front of your heart, or a hamsa hand or cross protecting you.

Using your thumb to mentally place a blue cross on the aggressor will return the hostile energy to its sender. Accompany this action with a wish that the attacker be cured of his or her anger. Reciting the mantra, "Om hreeng kleeng Krishnaya namaha" or something similar will accomplish this.

Be very, very careful with rebounding negative energy back towards it source. It may work in the short term, but in the long term it perpetuates the well-known cycle of attack, defense, and retaliation.

Always protect yourself, but do so with love for yourself as well as your "enemy". Shielding can also be as simple as having a loved one around whom stabilizes and protects your energy.

Crystals.

For those drawn to stones, using crystals may become a favorite method for auric cleaning. Many stones are said to benefit the aura, and simply holding a piece or being around them can help. Those with a greater interest in this area may want to learn more complicated techniques and how to lay stones on the body in specific ways.

Smoky quartz helps remove negative energy, and rose quartz helps replace negative energy with positive. Most dark colored stones, including black tourmaline and apache tears, are both grounding and good at repelling negative energies.

Fluorite and bloodstone clean the aura in general. If you choose to use this method, be sure to purify the stones before using them, and clean them regularly after they have been used several times. This can be done by burying them in earth overnight, placing them under running water, or putting them in salt.

Learning To Say "No" & Set Boundaries

This is a very concrete intervention, but your aura will thank you. Having a weak field is simply a reflection of a person's inability to protect themselves. At some point in their development, the person decided it was ok to let other people invade their space.

We have all met people who let this happen, as well as those who do not. If you want a strong aura, you cannot keep on giving into others' wishes, desires, and demands. You must learn to be strong within yourself, and be firm about where you energies and attention is directed.

Breathing Exercises

The entire system can be shifted through the manipulation of the breath, and this can also help the health of the aura. A yogic technique, called "kapalabhati", which means "shining skull breath", is beneficial to the system on multiple levels. It expels excess energy from the system, as well as increases circulation, tones the belly, and clears the sinuses.

To do this exercise:

1. Sit in a comfortable cross legged position with an erect spine, or upright in a straight-backed chair.

2. Sharply and quickly exhale through your nose, feeling your abdomen contract. Passively inhale, and allow your lungs to fill without effort.

3. Then, force the air out through the nostrils again.

Start slowly, both in pace and number of repetitions. Starting out with three rounds of ten exhales is fine. Eventually, this can be done for approximately five minutes at a time. Stop if you become lightheaded, and avoid this practice if you have a hernia, high blood pressure, or history of heart attack.

Bathing

Special baths have a similar impact to smudging when the right materials are used. Soaking in a tub with sea salt or baking soda cleans both the aura and the physical body. Visualization of releasing negative energy into the water can be added during the bath to increase the impact. Adding dried sage to the bath water is another option.

Aromatherapy

Certain scents affect the functioning of the system,

and some smells are good for auric health. Peppermint clears negative energy and prevents excess absorption. Cypress and juniper are also good at clearing bad vibes and sandalwood is excellent for overall harmony.

Cutting Cords

Regularly severing cords is an efficient way to improve your aura's health. It can be done regularly, or directly following a negative interaction. Some schools of thought even suggest doing it once or twice a day.

To do it:

1. Simply visualize all the cords coming from your body, starting with the front.

2. Focus your attention on releasing the ones that are not serving a positive purpose. Mentally gather them together, and imagine

cutting through them and casting them out of your field.

3. Any remnants of cord attached to your body can be mentally dissolved.

You may wish to knot the bundle prior to cutting, or pull the cord out directly from your own energetic field. If you do the latter, some like to patch the hole with light. After the front is done, repeat the same steps with the back.

If done correctly, you will experience a sense of lightness and clarity. This exercise can also be directed specifically towards cutting an unhealthy cord, or used consciously to help terminate a relationship when it comes to an end.

Sound Healing

Everything in the universe is a vibration, and we can alter our states by tuning into frequencies of greater harmony. Instruments like singing bowls and tuning forks clear the field, and some healing practitioners work specifically with sound as medicine. Mantra recitation is powerful, and there are many recordings of healing frequencies available online (search for "healing frequency" on Youtube, for example).

Withdraw Your Energy

As previously mentioned, the auric field extends three to four feet outside the average human. If you find yourself around negative influences — and do not wish to share and absorb their energy — simply withdraw your energy to prevent the fields from overlapping. This can be done physically by not shaking hands or making eye contact, and/or you can mentally draw your field in closer to the body to stop unwanted interactions.

Emotional & Historical Release

Repressed emotions are a huge cause of disease. Most diseases can be linked largely or partially to unresolved emotions. Instead of being acknowledged or expressed, they become lodged in the tissues and lead to stagnation. Nursing negative emotions is just as toxic, and creates an excess.

Releasing these is highly beneficial to your entire system, and will help clear the aura. Energy medicine automatically makes these surface, as the energetic flow is increased and the body is balanced.

Other options are journaling, traditional psychotherapy, and dance. Just talking about your feelings and allowing yourself to cry can do the trick. Past life regression therapy is taking the intervention further, by becoming aware of old events and situations and releasing them. This also clears the aura of old, stagnant information not pertinent to current functioning.

Mindset

Often when we have problems, we think treatment involves focusing on the symptoms. This is not always so. Being happy, grateful, and content works wonders for our health, and naturally cleans the aura of negativity. Laughter is proven to be highly beneficial for disease, and breaks up blockages in the system.

Cleaning the aura is an excellent practice, but there will be no long-term benefits if there is not a shift in attitude as well. We attract energy into our lives by virtue of our thoughts. If we think of ourselves as frail or persecuted, we are generating thoughts that weaken our aura. If we attack others physically or mentally, we are welcoming the same energy into *our* lives as well.

Chapter 9:

Strength & Health

Clearing the aura is a step in the right direction. Doing this regularly can help strengthen the field by itself, but there are additional options that are even more proactive in nature.

Harmonious Living

In general, having a healthy lifestyle supports good health of the auric field, and the more spiritually developed you are, the brighter, stronger, and larger the field. Poor diet, little exercise, negative thinking, living out of harmony with nature, lack of sleep, stress, destructive emotions, poor language (both malicious profanity and speaking ill of others in general), drugs, alcohol, and tobacco, and being around negative situations and people darken the aura.

Adopting wholesome habits and a positive attitude will automatically transform auric health over time. Sometimes, this is all that is required. Cleaning the aura regularly is a good idea, and should produce noticeable improvements, but will do nothing in the long run if the basics are not mastered. Clearing exercises and establishing a healthy lifestyle should be done simultaneously, for the best results.

Keeping the Company of Positive Influences

Choosing to stay close to positive people is wonderful for auric strength. This means surrounding yourself not only with people you like, but being picky about those whom you consider *healthy* to be around. It is being conscious about the company you keep, and deciding to be around those who are spiritually nourishing.

When you do this, you are exchanging energy with much more positive souls who have benevolent motivations. This may mean limiting contact with — or in some cases, even completely cutting ties with — those who drain you.

Meditation & Prayer

Meditation and prayer purifies. It is that simple. Engaging in these activities is like psychic surgery, in which the lowest parts of our nature are removed, and then replaced with higher vibrations. Some people have a set routine, and may attend a church, mosque, or temple, while others worship in their own way. Doing this strengthens and expands the aura.

If you are new to meditation, it is best to start with something simple (but still powerful) like a breathing meditation. Continual practice of this type of meditation (most commonly known as mindfulness) will help quiet your mind, which in turn will make you more sensitive to receiving subtle information.

To start:

1. Find a quiet and peaceful place where you are not at risk of being disturbed.

2. Find a comfortable place to sit, with your spine straight. Whether you sit on top of some pillows, a mat or in a chair is not important at this stage, as long as you keep your spine straight and you are not distracted from uncomfortable bodily sensations, like aching muscles or a constricted blood flow.

3. It is a good idea to start off the session with three long, exaggerated breaths to help prepare your mind for what's to come. Close your eyes fully or partially, and take a long, deep breath. Hold that breath for 3 or 4 seconds and then exhale fully. When you exhale, imagine all the stress and tension in your body and mind leaving with your breath. Repeat this step 3 times.

4. Now, allow yourself to breathe naturally. Focus on the sensations of the breath, your

chest and shoulders subtly rising and falling, the feeling of air entering your nose or mouth, the air filling your lungs etc. Keeping your focus on your breath is the crux of this meditation.

5. When you first start off, you'll probably find your mind wandering away from your breath from time to time. Instead of holding onto and judging these thoughts, simply let them go, and bring your attention back to your breathing.

With practice, this tendency of disorganized activity will be greatly reduced or even eliminated, and you will be much less affected by distractions and chaotic thought patterns. A quiet mind is a powerful baseline for which you can do further spiritual work.

Chanting & Affirmations

Chanting and toning sacred syllables changes the

energetic makeup of the body as well. It heals, protects and strengthens when used properly and when it's coming from the heart. It focuses the mind, and can also be a form of devotion.

The use of affirmations is another wonderful tool. They can be simple, such as, "I am light", or be a more complicated verse recited daily to remind you of what really matters. They can be targeted specifically to work with the auric field, or be more general and uplifting in nature.

Make Contact With Saints or Deities

This practice may seem strange to most Westerners, but it is actually found worldwide. In countries like India, it is common for devotees to keep pictures of their teacher, other mystical figures, or gods. These saints and deities are often prayed to and called upon for assistance, in both earthly and spiritual matters.

Some may say this is a psychological mechanism, but

most metaphysical wisdom teaches us that highly evolved beings are constantly at work in the affairs of mankind, and are here to help.

While they may not be bound to any particular religion or tradition, these entities will often take on forms familiar to the individual who calls for their aid. Establishing a relationship with one can provide the most powerful protection possible.

Having a relationship with Jesus or praying to the saints is the same. Find something that works within your own, personal spirituality.

Physical Exercises

In addition to the spiritual and mental techniques, there are physical movements that are said to be able to boost the aura as well.

The following yogic exercise uses the swinging of the arms to activate the aura and move the energy within it:

1. Sit in a comfortable seated position with a straight back. Make sure there is enough room around you to freely move your arms.

2. Begin with your arms straight at your sides. Bend the arms at the elbows so the forearms are in front of you at a 90-degree angle. Palms should face up. Cup the hands slightly.

3. As you inhale, draw the elbows back 6-12 inches.

4. And, as you exhale, bring the arms forwards and cross the arms in front of you, or loosely across the chest as if you were going to hug yourself.

5. As you inhale, draw the elbows back again, and this time, swing the arms straight all the way back.

6. Exhale and swing the straight arms (keep a slight bend in the elbow) up over the head.

7. Inhale to draw the elbows back and continue the sequence for a minute or two.

You can begin slowly, but it is most efficient when done more quickly. Increase your speed as you become more comfortable with the movement.

Doing Good Deeds

Referred to in Hinduism as "karma yoga", this is the practice of purification through good works. Performing selfless service destroys bad deeds and creates good energy. The most important thing any one of us can do is to accumulate good karma. It heals both ourselves and our fellow human beings.

It is a necessary part of any spiritual purification, and will thus strengthen the aura. It can be volunteer work, a random act of kindness, or just putting that extra bit of effort into home life, a relationship, or work.

Spending Time In Nature

It has been known for many years that contact with nature is healing, and living in noisy, polluted and tightly-packed cities is harmful to health. Many imbalances can be corrected or prevented by being in a more natural environment. Making time to do so will naturally align the body.

Living in congested communities is also hard on your energy, because it is overlapping and interacting with so many other fields. The human system was not intended to withstand such a high number of insults, and going to a place where there are fewer interactions gives your system a much-needed break.

Solitude

Healthy relationships can be key in healing yourself, but so can solitude. Most people need more of one than the other but, either way, solitude can be very powerful for personal development. If you have a hard time being alone, doing so is an especially important exercise. It gives you the opportunity to become aware of your *self*, and gain insight about who you are when not interacting in the usual relationships.

Taking a break from contact with others allows you to become more aware of patterns, and also helps separate what vibrations are your own and what vibrations are coming from others.

The aura is the first line of defense against any external energy. Just like any other part of the system, it can function well or poorly, can be flowing or stagnant. It is also possible for it to be damaged as a result of physical, emotional, or spiritual traumas. If you are having problems with immunity, balance, and protection, try cleaning and strengthening the aura. If the issues persist, it is possible that the aura needs to be repaired.

The wounds may be small or large, and vary in degrees of seriousness. Minor tears are easier to repair, and should close up naturally using the previous techniques. But if nothing is working, the damage may require more attention. It is completely possible to be doing everything "right" in your attempts to heal, and still make very little progress.

You could have good lifestyle habits, maintain a positive attitude, and use different healing methods in the attempt to overcome your symptoms. None of that will make much of an impact if the aura itself is compromised, because your energy is constantly leaking out while foreign energy is entering.

Working with all these tools can actually be counterproductive because of how confusing and frustrating it is. It can also be time consuming and expensive. Having a wounded auric field is like being in a boat with a hole in the bottom. Healing methods may bail the water out of the boat momentarily, but it will still continue to sink.

Injuries to the aura and system at large have an amazing way of appearing in the physical body also. There are multiple accounts of people who have past life memories of who they were and how they died.

An incredible synchronicity lies in the presence of

birth marks. If the person remembered having a death involving trauma to the body, they would often have a birth mark at the site of the past life injury (See the work of Dr. Ian Stevenson).

These people were sometimes able to remember their former identity, and confirm through public records or accounts from those who knew their previous incarnation how their former self died. The placement of their current birth mark and site of the wound during their previous incarnation matched.

Remember, the physical and subtle bodies are reflections of the other. Disease shows up in the subtle body first, and physical symptoms can be prevented from manifesting if the subtle body is addressed and its health is maintained. If you suspect there is a tear in the aura, try to see and/or sense the aura using the previously mentioned exercises.

Take your time and examine the field, looking for any tears or weak areas. If you find them, don't panic. That will only make them worse. Examine the area and see if there are any details or defining characteristics. Listen to your intuition about the best course of action.

Sealing the aura can be done on your own, but sometimes it is best to see a professional. There are many different modalities to choose from, including pranic healing, naturopathy, Traditional Chinese Medicine, Ayurveda, reiki, and gemstone healers. A good healer will be able to accurately diagnose the problems and give the appropriate treatment.

Doing this can save a great deal of time and suffering. If this is not practical, or if you believe it is something you must figure out on your own, set forth a clear intention before you begin.

Calling upon a higher power to help you make the best decision is never a bad idea. People sometimes experience miraculous healings that happen from a place of surrender, without any special tools or techniques. Take some time and look deeply into the different methods available to heal auric damage, and experiment with what works best.

With all of these options, it can be hard to know where to start. The paradoxical truth of the situation is that the more you chase something, the farther away it becomes. It is only when we combine appropriate action and an openness to let what we need come to us that we triumph. It is the difficult balance of setting the intention of what you want and letting it go with the faith that it will happen.

Trying too hard will get you nowhere, and is sending out a message of desperation to your body. It shows a lack of trust, and will damage your aura further. Experimenting is almost always necessary, but trying too many things is a sign that you lack focus.

Making a choice, even if it is the wrong one, is at least being decisive, and this will create confidence. The choice itself is less important than the *mindset*. Even if what you decide upon does not yield the results you hoped for, the fact that you were willing to dive in will eventually lead you to what you need. As the saying goes, "those who seek, shall find".

Conclusion

The human aura is a miraculous, complicated thing. It is truly a small universe by itself, and knowing this is both awe-inspiring and humbling. Learning to explore subtle forms of energy wakes us up to the magnitude of experience and makes us wonder what lies beyond.

Though the urban legend, "We only use 10 percent of our brains", is scientifically inaccurate, there is truth in what it is trying to convey: The human has massive amounts of energy in their system and a great deal of power at their fingertips. But, instead of exploring and tapping into our abundance, we choose to live in very limited, primitive ways.

Witnessing energy can be a wake-up call to how the universe really works, and a push in the direction towards expansion.
The wise Sufi poet Rumi once said, "Sell your cleverness and buy bewilderment". Should you choose to use this information to investigate yourself

and the cosmos, try to adopt this attitude.

Let go of what you think you know and how you perceive reality to be, and open yourself up to a whole new world of possibilities.

Printed in Great Britain
by Amazon